CULTIVATING YOUR CAREER

Planting the Seeds of Success for Professional Growth

SHAWNA MARTIN

Shawna Martin-- 1st ed.
Chief Editor, Shannon Buritz
ISBN: 978-1-954757-46-2

The Publisher has strived to be as accurate and complete as possible in the creation of this book.

This book is not intended for use as a legal, business, accounting, or financial advice source. All readers are advised to seek the services of competent professionals in legal, business, accounting, and finance fields.

Like anything else in life, there are no guarantees of income or results in practical advice books. Readers are cautioned to rely on their judgment about their individual circumstances to act accordingly.

While all attempts have been made to verify information provided in this publication, the Publisher assumes no responsibility for errors, omissions, or contrary interpretation of the subject matter herein. Any perceived slights of specific persons, peoples, or organizations are unintentional.

To my boys, John, Jake, and Tyler – my joys, my loves, my life – everything I do is because of and for you.

To all my parents – your constant love, encouragement, and support have been instrumental throughout my education and career. To my mom and her work family, thank you for the inspiring example of building strong connections and community in the workplace.

To all of the amazing advocates and mentors I had along my career journey: Kay, Wanda, Monique, and Sharon, whose early confidence in my abilities opened doors. And to my amazing JLL advocates: Bill, Eddy, Greg, Dave, Clark, Yishai, Amit, and Traci— thank you for your encouragement and support throughout my career journey.

To my girls, your unwavering support, despite any distance or time that separated us, has been a constant source of strength. You've been my confidants, always cheering me on and offering encouragement throughout every stage of life. Thank you for always being there for me and for putting up with my love of musicals and Taylor Swift ;)

Finally, to all of my peers, colleagues, and team members, you made the journey and experience worth it. You were the reason I came to work with joy, even amidst pressures, politics, and constant changes. And to those colleagues who became lifelong friends, I am so grateful for the opportunity to have worked alongside you and build friendships that will last a lifetime.

CONTENTS

CONTENTS

FOREWORD

Dear Reader,

I am thrilled to introduce you to Shawna Martin's exceptional book. Shawna is one of the few people I've encountered in my career who is both supremely capable and genuinely kind– a rarity amongst executives. Unsurprisingly, she's written a book focused on three pillars that span both the individual and the collective: Confidence, Culture, and Connection. She lays out a multifaceted approach to career growth, which compounds over time. This approach focuses on achieving personal success by uplifting others in their careers.

When I started working with Shawna, I was immediately struck by her deep experience leading teams, commitment to the people on her teams, integrity, and trust she built with everyone across a huge Fortune 200 multinational company. Everyone knew and respected Shawna Martin. This book embodies her hard-earned wisdom and commitment to empowering professionals like you.

The significance of the subjects Shawna has chosen to focus on in this book cannot be overstated. Too often, we're taught in business to have a winner-take-all mentality. Shawna's recommendations are quietly revolutionary because they push aside those highly individualistic approaches to career growth and instead focus on a more powerful interconnected approach. Confidence is the bedrock of any successful career, acting as the key that opens doors to new opportunities and challenges. Culture within the workplace shapes your daily experiences and others'; it can either foster collective growth or hinder collective progress. Lastly, connection with others not only enriches your professional journey but also amplifies your achievements through shared efforts and mutual support.

What makes Shawna's insights so crucial for today's professionals? In an era where the workplace is rapidly changing, work feels disconnected and alienating, and career paths are often non-linear, understanding how to navigate these changes confidently, adapt to or reshape organizational cultures, and forge meaningful connections is more important than ever. Shawna addresses these themes with practical advice and real-world examples that resonate with anyone looking to advance their career.

Why should you care about this book? Because it's not just about climbing the corporate ladder; it's about doing so in a way that stays true to your values and builds a mutual aid network along the way. It creates a much more fulfilling, sustainable model for career growth. Shawna empowers you to build a career that not only fulfills your ambitions but also contributes to a healthier, more inclusive professional environment.

I encourage you to read this book not just as a guide but as a conversation with a trusted mentor. Shawna's voice, expertise, and passion for career coaching are present on each page. I have had the privilege of Shawna's unique guidance and friendship over the years. In writing this book, she is making that available to so many more people.

Warm regards,
Tanya Koshy
Founder & CEO, Customer Science Collective
Product Leader & Advisor | ex-Meta, ex-Google

INTRODUCTION

Imagine your ideal future, where your career aspirations are no longer just dreams but tangible realities. Picture a world where you are not bound by the conventions of society, your workplace, or even the well-intentioned advice of friends and family, where your decisions are fueled by a deep understanding of your true desires and the things that bring you the most joy.

I encourage you to think beyond the confines of your current career journey. In my experience coaching individuals and leading teams, I've always emphasized the power of self-belief and the courage to pursue your passion. The journey towards achieving your dreams is not just about emotional fulfillment but also building a strong financial foundation to make those dreams a reality.

My goal is to equip you with the tools and mindset to achieve both. I firmly believe in the right to be rewarded fairly for your efforts. Pursuing dreams should be accompanied by the pursuit of recognition and fair compensation.

This book will empower you to believe in yourself, fight for the recognition you deserve, and boldly chase your dreams.

THE TRAP OF LIVING OTHERS' DREAMS

One of the most significant barriers my clients face is the pursuit of goals that aren't truly their own. It's easy to get caught up in what the world expects of us—climbing the corporate ladder, adhering to societal norms, or following paths laid out by others. This often leads to a profound sense of unfulfillment as they realize they've been chasing someone else's expectations, not their own.

The comfort of familiarity often holds people back from exploring new horizons. Having a mentor or role model in your journey can help you realize what you deserve and guide you toward change, overcoming common fears like rejection, whether asking for a raise, a new role, or a change in your career path. Pursuing your desires will often involve risks, so building your financial literacy and a strong financial foundation is essential to making bold decisions in your career and life.

SELF-ADVOCACY

You may be suspicious of those offering career advice. Does your company or manager genuinely have your best interests at heart? While it's natural to want to believe in our corporation's inherent goodness and support, the reality can sometimes be different. The hard truth is that, in many cases, companies and managers prioritize productivity and efficiency over their employees' individual growth and well-being.

This leads to an essential realization: you must become your own advocate. Trusting that a company will prioritize your personal career growth can be a risky assumption. You are responsible for fighting for your worth and success in the corporate world.

FOSTERING CONNECTIONS OVER COMPETITION

> *"A life well lived is not measured by the number of achievements, but by the depth of human connection."*
> - David Brooks, *The Second Mountain*

A common belief among corporate professionals is that their peers are competitors, constantly vying for the next promotion, project, or bonus. This perspective is limiting and can hinder long-term career growth. Instead of viewing colleagues as adversaries, embracing them as collaborators can lead to a more fulfilling and successful career. Authentic connections with peers enhance the work environment and open up opportunities for support, collaboration, and shared success. Breaking down the barriers of competition to build genuine relationships can transform the workplace into a source of joy and authenticity.

ADDRESSING YOUR CONCERNS ABOUT CAREER GROWTH

Through my interactions when leading teams and coaching individuals, I've identified several key questions that frequently arise regarding career growth and success. You may have many of the same questions.

- "How do I get my next role/promotion/raise?"
- "How do I deal with a difficult person or toxic culture?"
- "What should my next step be in my career?"

- "I'm burned out but feel stuck. What can I do to get unstuck?"
- "My job/career feels meaningless. I don't know if I want to do this for the rest of my life. What should I do?"
- "I'm underpaid and overworked. I can't remember why I chose this career. Help!"

My two decades in corporate technology, achieving roles of CIO and Executive Director, have given me a wealth of experience and insights into the corporate world's complexities and the answers to these commonly asked questions. Leading large international teams and spearheading major technology initiatives has shown me the importance of self-advocacy and personal passion in your career.

Despite my achievements and the support of wonderful colleagues, I often reflect on how my corporate experience could have been even more fulfilling. This realization drives my current mission: to be the guide and encourager I once needed. My greatest moments were not just in achieving personal success but in uplifting others in their career paths.

In the following pages, we will explore how CONFIDENCE, CULTURE, and CONNECTION are instrumental to your personal and professional growth and achievement.

DEFINING SUCCESS

The definition of success varies widely, reflecting the diversity of people's goals and life situations. Success could mean finding a role that brings more joy and fulfillment, achieving financial independence, or even the courage to leave a toxic work environment. It

SHAWNA MARTIN

might be about finding joy outside of work rather than within the day-to-day grind. The beauty is that success is not a one-size-fits-all concept. Each individual I work with has unique goals and desired outcomes that resonate with their values and aspirations.

The motivation for writing this book is simple: I want every reader to feel like they have a coach and mentor. Many find themselves navigating the corporate world alone. My vision is for you to realize that you are not alone in facing corporate challenges and gain the tools necessary to focus on what truly matters in your career - your passions, desires, and personal growth. I want you to feel supported, encouraged, and connected on this career journey.

- Shawna Martin

PART ONE

CONFIDENCE

CHAPTER ONE

BUILDING YOUR CONFIDENCE

*"Your success will be determined by your
own confidence and fortitude."*
- Former First Lady, Michelle Obama

How does confidence contribute to an accomplished and rewarding career? Think of confidence as the key that unlocks doors to opportunities. It propels you to submit your resume for that dream job, ask for the raise you deserve, pursue significant projects, and speak up in meetings. Confidence empowers you to seek and embrace feedback, recognize when it's time for a change, and step away from toxic environments.

Confidence answers those nagging questions: "Can I do this job? Am I worth this money? Am I good enough?" I'm here to tell you unequivocally *you are*. You're capable, deserving, and more than enough. Through this book, I aim to help you realize that you possess everything you need for a successful career and to build the confidence to make it a reality.

Let's define **confidence**, particularly in career growth. Merriam-Webster describes it as "a feeling or consciousness of one's powers or of reliance on one's circumstances." When turned inwards, this feeling is **self-confidence**: "confidence in oneself and in one's powers and abilities."

Confidence provides the motivation and internal support to pursue what's right for you in your career. While it may seem like some people are brimming with confidence, remember that most people, at some point, second-guess themselves. You're not alone in needing that nudge to take the next step.

In this chapter, you will gain a deeper understanding of confidence, its impact on your career, and practical ways to cultivate and harness it to shape your path to achievement.

TRANSFORMATIVE MOMENTS IN CAREER JOURNEYS

Confidence can impact career success, compensation, and recognition in many ways. Consider a colleague of mine who stepped into a larger team. Unsure about her salary compared to her peers, she mustered the courage to ask her manager about it. Just by inquiring if she was being paid fairly, she was granted a 10% raise to align with her colleagues. While outcomes like this aren't guaranteed, the simple step of asking the question requires confidence.

Another story is of a young client aspiring to be a manager. By confidently expressing her ambitions and concerns to her manager, she made her career goals known. Coinciding with a reorganization, she was offered a supervisor role just six months later, setting her on the path to becoming a first-time manager. This is a testament to how confidently expressing your aspirations can align opportunities with your goals.

SHAWNA MARTIN

OVERCOMING BARRIERS TO CONFIDENCE

Confidence, believe it or not, is a universal challenge. It often appears that others have it in abundance, but most people struggle with it internally, whether it shows on the outside or not.

One effective way to build confidence is through support from someone you trust, a mentor or a confidant. This person can provide feedback and encouragement and share their experiences, which can be incredibly empowering. Choose someone who is genuinely invested in your success. This book is a part of that support system, sharing experiences and wisdom to help bolster your confidence. You're not alone in this journey.

When facing a confidence hurdle, weigh the best and worst outcomes. For instance, the best outcome in asking for a raise would be getting that immediate raise! The worst outcome could be a "no," but the potential for positive change makes it a risk worth taking. Understanding the various possible outcomes can significantly boost your courage to take action.

Embracing the Learning Curve

Remember the old saying, "Practice makes perfect?" It's especially true for confidence. The more you put yourself out there, the more you'll see results that bolster your confidence. Feeling apprehensive about things you are trying for the first time is normal. Use positive self-talk, take a deep breath, and take the leap. It doesn't mean you will always get it right or never make mistakes, but you will continue to learn and grow with each experience.

In any career, facing failures and rejections is inevitable. How you handle these moments can significantly impact your confidence and career trajectory. Always remember to:

- **Be gentle with yourself.** Everyone makes mistakes, and these missteps don't spell the end of your career or diminish your overall contributions. Acknowledge the mistake, but don't let it define you.

- **Take a moment to breathe and reflect.** The goal isn't to dwell on the mistake but to consider what you can learn from the experience. How would you handle a similar situation in the future? What lessons can you take away to improve and grow?

- **Consider the source of feedback.** Criticism is usually more of a reflection of the critic's biases than your capabilities. As Nelson Mandela wisely said, "I learned that courage was not the absence of fear, but the triumph over it. The brave man is not he who does not feel afraid, but he who conquers that fear." Strive to face challenges, including criticism, with courage and resilience.

- **Seek support.** A mentor, coach, or trusted confidant can help you see that one person's negative words are not a definitive reflection of your worth or abilities. Mark Twain advised, "Keep away from people who try to belittle your ambitions. Small people always do that, but the really great make you feel that you, too, can become great." Surround yourself with individuals who uplift and inspire you.

SHAWNA MARTIN

THE INTERSECTION OF SELF-ASSURANCE, SELF-WORTH, AND CONFIDENCE

Confidence, self-assurance, and self-worth are deeply interconnected. When you're confident in your abilities and knowledge, it reflects in your interactions, presentations, and the solutions you provide. This assurance doesn't just benefit you; it's evident to your peers and leaders, contributing positively to your professional image.

A critical aspect of self-worth in the workplace is ensuring you're fairly compensated and recognized for your contributions. This process starts with self-confidence. Believe in your value, and don't hesitate to advocate for yourself. As you progress through this book, consider how you can apply the tips and habits to your daily work routine. Each piece of advice is a stepping stone to building a more confident, assured, and valued professional self.

THE SPECTRUM OF CONFIDENCE

It's common to encounter colleagues who seem to exude confidence effortlessly. However, I always encourage my clients to remember that everyone has their unique journey. That seemingly confident person might be "faking it till they make it," benefiting from excellent mentorship, or coming from a background that naturally nurtured their confidence. Don't let someone else's confidence diminish your own. You are your own person with unique value and contributions.

On the flip side, there's overconfidence, which often manifests as arrogance or dismissiveness. Reflect on how you perceive individuals who exhibit overconfidence. Generally, overconfidence is viewed negatively, perceived more as arrogance than strength. This perception is crucial to remember as you navigate your professional life.

In your journey to build confidence, always aim to couple it with respect, collaboration, and support. Your goal is to confidently bring your knowledge and expertise into the workplace without crossing into the territory of arrogance.

SOUNDING BOARDS FOR GROWTH

Very few people I know or have coached are born with innate confidence. Mentorship and coaching are pivotal in building confidence, as it is nurtured over time. A mentor or coach acts as a sounding board, helping you work through scenarios, reminding you of your accomplishments, and building confidence in your value. My clients have worked through imposter syndrome, learned to communicate their neurodivergent needs and strengths, and cultivated cultural connections in their workplaces despite discrimination, exclusion, and long-held insecurities. They walk away from each session with courage, comfort, and a clear understanding of who they are.

TAKE YOUR NEXT STEP POWERFULLY

As you continue on your career path, take each step with confidence. Confidence is not about perfection but growth, learning, and resilience. It's about knowing your value and stepping forward, even in the face of uncertainty. I hope you carry with you the knowledge that your confidence, continually nurtured and developed, will be one of your greatest assets in your professional journey.

SHAWNA MARTIN

KEY TAKEAWAYS

ଔ Confidence is essential for career growth, empowering you to pursue opportunities, ask for what you deserve, and handle change with assurance.

ଔ Developing confidence involves seeking mentorship, embracing feedback, and learning from successes and setbacks.

ଔ Practicing confidence through actions, like asking for a raise or expressing career goals, often leads to tangible progress and self-improvement.

ଔ Overcoming fears and handling failures with grace are integral to building lasting confidence.

ଔ Balancing confidence with humility is key, ensuring that self-assurance does not turn into overconfidence.

CHAPTER TWO

FINDING YOUR PASSION

It's a story many of us know all too well. You finish college armed with a degree and a bundle of hope. You snag a job that seems perfect—interesting work, decent pay. But before you know it, you're trapped in the relentless grind of corporate life. You learn the game: how to climb the ladder, snag raises and bonuses, and what it takes to get promoted. Yet, in this rush, it's so easy to lose sight of what drew you to your field in the first place.

In the hustle of corporate life, one question often falls by the wayside: Do you love what you're doing? We work to live, not the other way around. But sometimes, that's forgotten as we chase what we're told is success. I want this book to guide you back to your true passions, not just the ones your job or society dictates.

> *"Success is liking yourself, liking what*
> *you do, and liking how you do it."*
> - Maya Angelou

Finding joy in your work might seem like a tall order, but it's far from impossible. You might need to lay down a financial base or prioritize other life goals first, but I encourage you to find at least part of what brings you joy in your work. Are you in an environment where you feel valued? Do you get recognition for your hard work? You don't have to love every aspect of your job. Sometimes, the people, the culture, and the little victories make your day-to-day rewarding.

If you're ending your weeks exhausted, feeling lost, or undervalued, it's time for some introspection. These are signs that your job isn't serving you well. Work is a part of life, not its entirety. You deserve a career that energizes you, not leaves you drained. Striking a balance between your professional and personal life is key. Find a role that aligns with your values, where you can end your day feeling fulfilled and still have the energy to enjoy life outside of work. We spend a significant portion of our lives at work. Why settle for a job that doesn't spark joy, personal growth, and satisfaction or reward you generously for your effort?

THE CEO'S QUESTION

I remember when a CEO, amidst a massive organizational reshuffle, gave me the opportunity to select my next career path. The vast options – from product management to operations to customer engagement – reflected my experience and seniority. But the question he asked that really struck me was, "What do you want to wake up every day doing? What is your passion?"

At that point in my career, I had always focused on what seemed like the next logical step: identifying gaps and stepping in to fill them. Being adept at identifying and resolving complex problems was, undoubtedly, part of my passion. However, when asked about what I loved doing the most, I was at a loss. My career had been shaped by my readiness to tackle new challenges, but I hadn't paused to consider what truly ignited my passion. This moment of uncertainty led me to a period of deep reflection. I took time for myself and reached out to mentors, confidants, and encouragers.

I realized I was tired of the front-line, client-facing roles and all the politics that came with them (not that politics don't exist in any executive role). I truly loved leading a team, nurturing careers, and solving operational problems. This insight allowed me to build a product operations team from the ground up, focusing on areas I was passionate about and addressing challenges that would benefit the entire organization.

EMBRACING YOUR CAREER PASSION

My own career taught me a valuable lesson, even though it was later than I would have liked: the importance of regularly asking yourself, "Am I enjoying what I'm doing?" I hope this encourages you to reflect on your career path.

Realizing what you truly enjoy in your career might not be straightforward, especially if you're unsure about your passion. Numerous tools and methods can help you explore, try, and learn. Don't hesitate to ask for feedback. Find out what others think you excel at. But remember, just because you're good at something doesn't mean it's your calling. Think about the parts of your day that bring you the most joy. Is it mentoring a colleague, solving a complex engineering problem, or crafting and presenting a strategy? These moments, no matter how small, can be powerful indicators of where your passion lies.

> *"Passion is energy. Feel the power that comes from focusing on what excites you."*
> - Oprah Winfrey

It's never too late to ask yourself if you're truly happy with what you're doing. And if the answer is no, it's entirely within your power to shape your career to bring out the best in you and allow you to share that best with the world.

SHAWNA MARTIN

KEY TAKEAWAYS

၈ Reflect regularly to stay connected with your true passions, ensuring your job aligns with what fulfills you.

၈ Strive to find aspects of your job that bring happiness,
whether it's the people, culture, or tasks, as joy in work
contributes significantly to life satisfaction.

၈ A fulfilling career should energize rather than drain, allowing enjoyment in both professional and personal life.

၈ Being skilled at something doesn't mean it's your passion;
explore different job facets to discover what excites you.

၈ If your current job doesn't make you happy or align with
your values, you can change your career path to pursue
what brings out the best in you.

CHAPTER THREE

KNOWING YOUR WORTH

Have you ever experienced that gut-wrenching moment when you realize you're working your ass off, putting in all your effort, only to find out someone less skilled or less motivated is earning more than you? This is a harsh reality in many workplaces. Despite efforts to address pay disparities and compensation inequity, it's still shockingly common to see individuals earning less than their less qualified or less successful peers. So, what's the solution? It's simple but powerful: *Know your worth!*

Knowing your worth isn't just a matter of deciding the figure you want to see on your paycheck. It involves understanding what the market values, what other companies are paying, and what your peers are earning and evaluating whether the pay you receive is commensurate with the work, stress, and even the culture or toxic b***s*** you might have to put up with daily. This understanding helps determine whether it's worth staying in your current role or at your current company. Knowing your worth means recognizing and insisting on being rewarded and compensated fairly.

THE HARSH REALITY OF
COMPENSATION INEQUITY

One of the most eye-opening and, frankly, frustrating moments in my career occurred when I was promoted to an executive leadership position. With this promotion came the responsibility of overseeing new talent who were previously my peers. It was during this time that I encountered a startling revelation.

Upon assuming this role, I gained access to salary histories and discovered something unsettling. Several individuals on my team, who held lower titles and had a narrower scope of work than mine, had been earning significantly more than I had for years. Despite higher performance ratings and having the same boss, their compensation far exceeded mine, even though I was a step above in seniority and scope. Unfortunately, in many cases, a company's primary loyalty lies with its shareholders or bottom line, not always with its employees. They might offer compensation based on what they think you will accept rather than what you truly deserve.

Learning about the realities of the corporate world was a shock to the system. No matter how much I contributed to the company, my management team had not taken the necessary steps to ensure I was paid fairly and equitably. This experience was a turning point, and it instilled in me a firm resolve. I became adamant about advising everyone I work with and my entire professional network on the importance of fighting for what they deserve.

MASTERING THE ART OF NEGOTIATION

The best time to leverage negotiation is when you are stepping into a new position. When dealing with recruiters, be clear and confident, and don't shy away from negotiating beyond the first offer. As a hiring manager, I'll be honest - I've always respected those who countered the first offer. It showed confidence and a desire for fairness. It demonstrated that they knew their worth.

Once you've made it to the offer stage, the company has already invested time, money, and resources in selecting you and wants you to come on board. This is an incredible opportunity to use your leverage and make the money you deserve.

Here's a little insider secret: Almost every company has some wiggle room in their salary offerings. If they can't move on base salary, consider negotiating on other compensation or reward alternatives. Think about increasing annual bonuses, additional days off, company-sponsored conferences that enhance your career and networking opportunities, further training or skills development, or even having the company pay for a career coach. Attending conferences or training seminars can immensely benefit your career development and morale. Don't hesitate to ask for opportunities to attend these events and make these requests early, preferably before budget cycles are finalized. Bring up the importance of these opportunities during your performance reviews and discussions about your professional growth.

Similarly, if you're aiming for leadership roles, inquire about individualized leadership programs, development opportunities, and leadership coaching. These are investments in your career trajectory.

THE POWER OF ASKING

Let's address a common dilemma. What if you are already in a job and content with the company but uncertain if you are being paid fairly? The solution is straightforward: Ask! Make it a habit to inquire about your compensation during every review cycle, merit increase, and compensation review. And if doubts about fair pay arise mid-year, feel free to bring it up then, too.

There's absolutely no harm in asking. Reminding your manager or HR to assess your pay fairly is critical in ensuring your compensation aligns with your worth. Those who don't ask often find themselves stuck with minimal year-over-year merit increases. But what could happen if you do ask? The worst-case scenario is a simple "no," but you might be in for a positive surprise on the flip side. The number of people I know who have merely asked, "Am I being compensated fairly?" and subsequently received significant raises is astonishing. I've seen cases where this simple question led to a 5 to 10% increase. All it takes is the confidence and courage to ask.

For example, a close peer of mine was working in a new leadership role in her company, which had never existed before. It was a position without precedent, making establishing a clear benchmark for appropriate compensation challenging. However, a logical approach was to compare the role with others at a similar level, considering factors like the number of direct reports and overall scope.

An interesting thing happened when my peer questioned whether her pay was fair and equitable compared to her colleagues. Despite the absence of industry-specific benchmarks, the company responded. A few weeks later, she received a 10%

raise, aligning her compensation with her peers. This instance is a prime example of the power and importance of simply asking the question.

Now, this doesn't mean you shouldn't do your research ahead of asking. While many companies discourage salary discussions among employees, I strongly advocate for transparency and honesty. Understanding what your peers and network earn, especially those in similar roles, is necessary to gauge your compensation. It's important to recognize that salary should reflect a standard range based on role and level, ensuring equity and fairness within the organization. Meanwhile, bonuses present an opportunity to reward high performers, allowing for additional compensation that reflects outstanding performance.

Explore platforms like Glassdoor, Level.fyi, and LinkedIn and reach out discreetly to trusted mentors for their insights on what your role should command regarding salary. Their responses might surprise you and bolster your confidence to negotiate what you're truly worth.

RECOGNIZING WHEN TO MOVE ON

If your employer is unwilling or unable to meet your fair compensation, it's time to consider a change. This decision can be tough, especially if you love your team or role. However, imagine the fulfillment of being in a job you love, surrounded by a great team, and receiving the compensation you deserve.

Continuing in a role where you're underpaid can profoundly impact your morale and sense of value. It's like a slow chip away at your soul, knowing that your efforts and contributions aren't being justly rewarded. You owe it to yourself to go after what you deserve.

YOUR WORTH, YOUR FUTURE

Make it a point to periodically assess whether you're doing work you love and feel fairly compensated for. Compensation is a large component of our career goals, passions, and the pursuit of financial freedom and security for ourselves and our families.

Never settle for what's simply offered. Have the confidence to demand fair and equitable pay for your contributions. Asserting your worth demonstrates that you respect your skills, time, and career journey. You are not just an employee; you are a valuable and integral part of the team.

KEY TAKEAWAYS

ଔ Know your worth beyond the paycheck by understanding market standards and evaluating the value of your role in terms of work, stress, and workplace culture.

ଔ In negotiations, especially for new positions, always ask for more and use resources like Glassdoor and LinkedIn to research fair compensation; remember, there's often wiggle room beyond the initial offer.

ଔ Regularly inquire about your compensation, particularly during review cycles and when doubts arise, as asking can lead to significant salary adjustments.

ଔ If your current employer can't meet your fair compensation expectations, have the courage to seek opportunities where your contributions are valued and rewarded equitably.

ଔ Continuously assess job satisfaction and compensation alignment, and advocate for your value in the workplace, never settling for less than you deserve.

CHAPTER FOUR

CLIMBING THE CORPORATE LADDER

The ladder is a familiar metaphor for career progression in the corporate world. Climbing this ladder can be fun, challenging, and incredibly rewarding. It's an opportunity to learn and grow in ways you never imagined. Throughout this chapter, we'll explore areas to help you build confidence as you move up. We'll uncover some of the less-discussed aspects of advancing to new levels, such as understanding your pay range, tackling imposter syndrome, knowing what's required for promotion, stepping into management, and collaborating with HR. Regardless of which step you choose to take on the corporate ladder, from being an individual contributor, a new manager, or even an executive, we'll cover it all.

> *"I am not a product of my circumstances.*
> *I am a product of my decisions."*
> - Stephen Covey, Author of *The 7*
> *Habits of Highly Effective People*

UNDERSTANDING THE RUNGS OF YOUR CAREER LADDER

The corporate world has numerous paths catering to different skills, aspirations, and career goals. From the foundational role of an individual contributor to the strategic position of an executive in the C-suite, each step on the corporate ladder presents its own challenges, opportunities for growth, and occasionally moments of doubt, commonly known as imposter syndrome.

As we progress through each stage of our careers, it's important to recognize the unique aspects of each rung on the ladder and how we can grow our confidence along the way. Let's explore each of these roles, starting with the individual contributor.

Mastery and Growth as an Individual Contributor

As an individual contributor, you're recognized as an expert in your domain. Your days are often filled with execution and delivery and improving your skills. It is important in this role to seek investment in your growth from your company. Whether training, licenses, exam fees, or certifications, don't hesitate to ask for support. It's always better to initiate these conversations than to wonder what might have been.

An aspect of the individual contributor role rarely discussed is the opportunity to advance to a senior level without transitioning into management. This pathway can be incredibly fulfilling for those who prefer to focus on the craft itself rather than on leading teams. Individual contributor roles can be rewarding and highly lucrative for those early in their careers.

The Multifaceted Role of a Manager

As a manager, your responsibilities extend beyond your goals and deliveries. You're now in charge of setting the vision for your team, defining expectations, and ensuring the collective success of your group. This means actively participating in each team member's career development, facilitating continuous learning opportunities, and offering the leadership support necessary to excel in their roles.

Becoming a manager also means embracing the emotional complexities of leadership. You'll encounter a range of personalities, aspirations, and challenges within your team. The key to navigating these dynamics lies in being a confident, compassionate, and collaborative leader. As a manager, you have the power to significantly influence your team members' joy and fulfillment in their work.

Stepping into management doesn't mean your learning journey comes to a halt. Instead, your focus shifts from mastering technical or trade-specific skills to acquiring strategic insights and relationship-building abilities. Understanding the contributions of cross-functional teams, fostering relationships with peers, and identifying growth opportunities for your team members become your new priorities.

You must advocate for your own development in these areas. While ideally, every organization would provide training for new managers and those leading larger teams, this is not always the reality. If formal support is lacking, take the initiative to seek learning opportunities yourself. This could mean reading books, seeking peer advice, or finding a coach or mentor to guide your growth.

As you face the complexities of management, building connections becomes increasingly important. These relationships will support your current role and pave the way for future opportunities. In subsequent chapters, we'll explore networking and relationship-building in greater depth.

The Surprising Reality of Executive Life

When you step into your new executive role, one of the first realizations that might catch you off guard is that everyone around you is still learning and growing. Even at this level, imposter syndrome can loom large, and the pressure to know it all can be intense. But here's a secret: nobody has all of the answers. This realization is both humbling and liberating. We're all human, each of us navigating our professional and personal development path. Embrace this truth, and let it reinforce your confidence. You've earned your spot at this table.

Tips for Success at the Executive Level

➢ **Master Negotiation**: Negotiation takes on a new level of significance at the executive level. Everything from your compensation package to the perks of having an executive assistant or a professional coach falls under this umbrella. It's also a time to be strategic about your employment terms, including aspects like severance agreements and equity compensation —elements potentially overlooked in the excitement of accepting a new role.

➢ **Understand Your Scope:** The scope of an executive's role can be surprisingly fluid, focusing heavily on strategic direction, corporate negotiations, and organizational politics. These responsibilities can shift based on broader firm priorities, so adapting as things evolve and having clear outcomes for yourself and your team is key.

➤ **Take Care of Yourself:** The demands of executive life can quickly sweep you into a relentless cycle of work, often at the expense of personal well-being. Remember, life extends beyond the office walls. Make time for hobbies, family, and self-reflection. Equally important is having a vision for your future, whether it involves retirement, board membership, entrepreneurship, or another venture. Continually reassess your passion and make choices that align with your true self.

HR IN THE WORKPLACE

As you climb the corporate ladder, understanding compensation ranges, career frameworks, performance ratings, bonus structures, and requirements for promotions is essential for you to move up and be fairly compensated for your work. Upon joining a new company, take the time to familiarize yourself with its HR frameworks. Many organizations assign an HR business partner to employees and teams. Building a relationship with your HR business partner can provide a go-to resource for questions and guidance. In your performance reviews and discussions, openly discuss your career aspirations and the steps needed to ascend to the next level. Sharing your passions and goals helps align your career trajectory with your personal ambitions and ensures you're on the same page with your manager regarding your growth.

THE SIGNIFICANCE OF CAREER FRAMEWORKS

Career frameworks are essential, especially within larger corporations, for matching the right skills to the right roles at the most effective cost to the company. Companies are driven by profitability and aim to allocate compensation efficiently, paying for the skills they need without overspending. This reality can be eye-opening for those who assume excellence in their current role will automatically lead to promotion.

A career framework outlines each role's specific skills and expectations and associated compensation ranges. Know where you stand and advocate for yourself when ready to take on more responsibility. You must recognize whether upward mobility is possible within your current team or if you need to seek opportunities elsewhere to advance.

I once worked with a manager who was deeply invested in her team's growth, aiming to promote her members. However, the organizational structure only needed specific roles at certain levels within her team, meaning for her team members to advance, they had to seek opportunities outside her team. This scenario illustrates the importance of understanding your company's career framework and the potential limitations within your current team structure.

CONTINUAL REEVALUATION AND CAREER PIVOTS

One piece of advice I cannot stress enough is the importance of continuously reevaluating your position on this path. It's far too easy to get caught up in the climb only to stop one day and question why you're here and where you're heading next. Reassess your career journey at various intervals. Are you following your passions or merely ticking off the boxes to the next step?

Pursuing career growth must go beyond external expectations. It's important to foster your own development, learn new skills, and maintain your motivation, passion, and joy in what you do. This is what keeps the journey exciting and fulfilling.

It's also vital to recognize when it might be time for a change. It is perfectly reasonable to pivot in your career journey, whether transitioning from a technical role to management, exploring a new industry, or taking a step back to reduce stress and enjoy life outside work. These pivots are normal and should be embraced as a healthy part of your career evolution.

FINDING YOUR TRUE FIT

Let's talk about a common misconception in the corporate world – that success only comes from climbing higher and higher. But what if I told you that true success, happiness, and fulfillment sometimes come from knowing when to pause? Reflect on where you want to be on the corporate ladder, not just where you can reach.

I once worked with someone who's a perfect example of this. He had reached the director level, a position many aspire to and work tirelessly to achieve. He went through the stressful process of panel interviews, preparations, and presentations, and finally, he made it to the top of his corporate ladder. Upon getting there, he realized it didn't align with his desires and passions. And that was perfectly okay. He gave leadership a chance, tried it out, and then confidently decided to take a step back. This decision is often met with resistance. We're seldom encouraged or supported to step down from leadership roles back to individual contributor positions. Yet, having the courage to prioritize personal fulfillment over conventional success is a strength, not a weakness.

If you find yourself in a similar situation, feeling that a senior individual contributor role suits you better, don't hesitate to make that change. Apply for roles that resonate with your passions, allowing you to engage deeply with the day-to-day work you love most. Ignore the potential judgment from others. After all, this is your life, career, and happiness at stake.

The individual who chose to step back? He's thriving, finding even more success by working in a role he is passionate about, and continues to be a leader among his peers outside of a traditional management role.

YOU'VE GOT THIS

Remember that you possess the skills, talent, and determination needed to impact the corporate world significantly. By following your passions, advocating for yourself, and understanding the corporate frameworks in place, you can achieve success with confidence. Believe in your ability to contribute meaningfully and advocate for fair compensation and recognition. Never lose sight of your worth and potential. The corporate ladder is yours to climb, equipped with the knowledge and resilience you've developed along the way. You've got this!

KEY TAKEAWAYS

ભ Continuously reassess your career path to ensure it aligns with your passions and not just the next step up the corporate ladder. Embrace career pivots as a healthy part of your evolution.

ભ Success isn't only about climbing higher; sometimes, it's about finding where you truly fit, even if it means taking a step back to focus on what brings you joy and fulfillment.

ભ Understand the significance of each role on the corporate ladder, from individual contributor to executive, and seek investment in your growth at every stage. Don't shy away from advocating for yourself.

ભ Building strong relationships with HR and understanding your company's career framework is crucial for navigating your path and being fairly compensated for your work.

ભ The corporate ladder is yours to climb, but making informed, passion-driven decisions is important. Never underestimate your worth and potential.

PART TWO

CULTURE

CHAPTER FIVE

SETTING YOUR WORK BOUNDARIES

"Why is culture so important to a business? Here is a simple way to frame it. The stronger the culture, the less corporate process a company needs. When the culture is strong, you can trust everyone to do the right thing."
- Brian Chesky, Co-founder and CEO, Airbnb

Culture is one of the most significant areas you can source and develop to bring joy and satisfaction to your career journey. Culture relates not only to the work environment in which you take a role but also to relationships around you, your team, your manager, and the work environment you create for yourself. It is essential to pursue a work culture you want to be a part of, to understand how company culture can affect your joy, well-being, and passions, and to discuss how you can contribute to building and supporting a positive work culture.

We'll start by learning how to create the type of work environment that supports you and allows you to have success and balance within your role. There are numerous articles, tips, and training around work boundaries. I want to focus on the bigger picture of work boundaries and how they relate to your well-being.

In the daily grind of life, it's easy to focus on urgent things and prioritize work above your own well-being. However, as the old adage goes, you only have this one life to live. As we discussed in the section about finding your passion, your work life and time must reflect those areas of priority for yourself.

When you think about workplace culture and boundaries, they are closely related. The culture and environment in which you work either safeguard or disrespect your boundaries. Consider what type of work environment you want to be in. It should support your priorities and help you be successful in your career and personal life. This may mean pursuing flexible work, finding a job that allows you to work remotely, adjusting work hours around kids' schedules, or having a supportive manager and team who care as much about you as a person as they do about your work contributions.

As you assess your passions and what you want from your career, reassess what you want out of your life. Prioritize the most important things to you and determine where work falls in that prioritization list. Make sure that your time reflects that prioritization of your life. Never put work ahead of yourself, your well-being, or your loved ones. Don't put off doctor's appointments, your health, or relationships to answer another email or schedule another meeting.

WORK PRIORITIZATION METHODS

Once you have a firm grasp on where work falls in the priorities of your life, next is prioritizing the work itself. There are dozens of methods for prioritizing work, and I encourage you to try as many as you are interested in and find what works for you. Here are a few of my favorites.

EISENHOWER METHOD

> *"Who can define for us with accuracy the difference between the long and short term! Especially whenever our affairs seem to be in crisis, we are almost compelled to give our first attention to the urgent present rather than to the important future."*
> - Dwight D. Eisenhower, 1961 Address
> to the Century Association

This method helps identify and separate tasks based on their importance and urgency. It creates a matrix to categorize each task, and based on which box it falls into, the matrix helps you assign the priority or know what step to take next for that particular task.

As you look through your list of tasks, you determine if they are important or not, urgent or not. Then, you focus on those that are both important and urgent first. For everything else, you either schedule for a later time or delegate. Delete anything that is not important and not urgent.

The Eisenhower Matrix

	Urgent	Not urgent
Important	**Do:** Tasks with deadlines or consequences.	**Schedule:** Tasks with unclear deadlines that contribute to long-term success.
Not important	**Delegate:** Tasks that must get done but don't require your specific skill set.	**Delete:** Distractions and unnecessary tasks.

asana

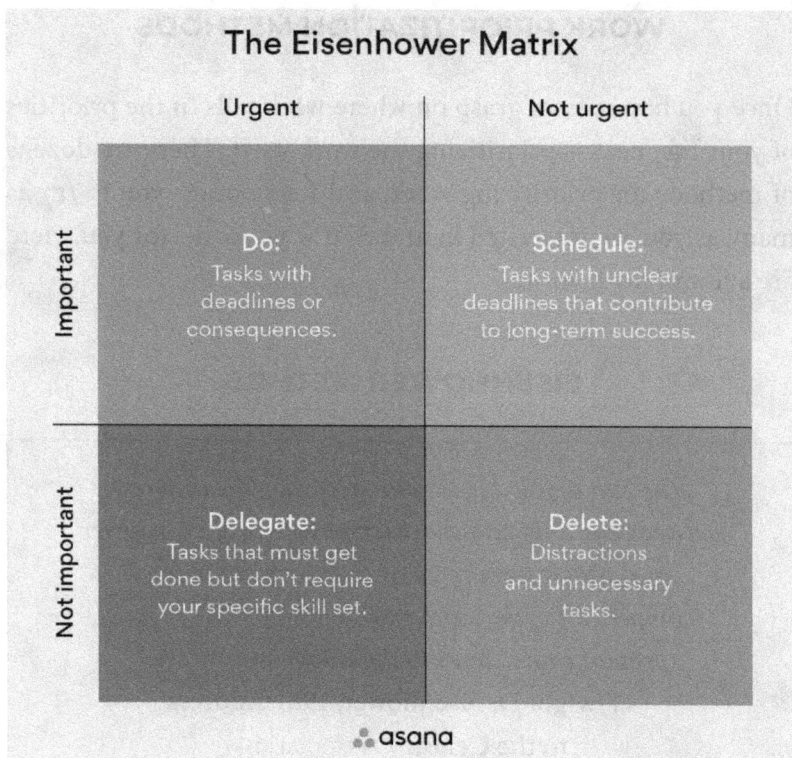

Credit: Asana.com

RULE OF THREE

The Rule of Three is a strategy that encourages you to identify the top three items that are most crucial to complete each day and do those first; if those three things are the only things you accomplish that day, fantastic! Anything else that happens is just icing on the cake. I like this method as it helps filter out the noise and provides a sense of accomplishment when those three things are done. It also helps, like the Eisenhower Method, to focus on the most urgent and important things. I also like doing this in my personal life, so I tend to have my top three items for work and my top three items for home. Sometimes, they don't all get done, and that's OK!

ZERO INBOX

> *"Do email less."*
> - Merlin Mann

Zero Inbox is a tool I found later in my career, and it became one of my preferred work prioritization methods. A productivity expert and author, Merlin Mann, created the Zero Inbox method in the early 2000s, which is still very useful today. The focus of this method is to spend less time doing email and more time on the strategic work in your day.

It is similar to the Eisenhower Method in that it encourages you to determine if the task is important to complete or can be delegated. The difference is that you make these decisions quickly as you respond to each email. Anything that takes less than a few minutes to respond to or delegate should be dealt with immediately. Items that don't require a response or action should be immediately archived or deleted. The necessary and urgent items can be scheduled and focused on as a priority. This method helps reduce the clutter that email can bring and frees time to focus on your day's priorities.

Regardless of your chosen method, be gentle with yourself and remember that this is a tool to help you prioritize work, not a report card on how well you use it. A tool may work one week but not the next, and that's okay. Try a different method or take a week off and return to it the following week. There is no right or wrong with these methods; it's just finding the one that works best for you at the given time.

SPEAKING OF DELEGATION...

Using delegation as an avenue for accomplishing a task is a critical skill to learn throughout your career. I once had an up-and-coming star performer on one of my teams, and the one area of continued growth I continually pushed them toward was practicing delegation. While there are times that it feels easier to do something yourself, over the long run, it is much easier if you can assist those around you who are capable of completing or taking over your tasks. If you are interested in moving up into management, you will have to learn to delegate, or you will burn yourself out or set yourself up for failure. Once the star performer on my team began truly delegating the tasks that could be accomplished by somebody else, they were able to focus much more on strategy and contributing at a higher level of leadership.

CREATING A SUSTAINABLE WORK-LIFE BALANCE

"Where you decide to put your time and attention says a lot about who you are as a human being."
- Merlin Mann

Work is not all we have in life; it's easy to get caught up in the corporate rat race, but most people remember the connections they've built with friends and loved ones and their relationships

SHAWNA MARTIN

throughout their lives. Not the last project they worked on or getting that next promotion.

Work with your managers to ensure you're on the same page of priorities. I encourage you to meet with your manager regularly to discuss the most important things to be completed. One of my coaching clients previously struggled with this due to her manager's communication style. She was ready at every one of their one-on-one check-ins but could never get the manager to focus on confirming her priorities and discussing her strategy to accomplish them. We found a solution to help her adjust to the manager's communication style by sharing her priorities and topics for discussion for their one-on-ones via email at least 24 hours ahead to help focus her manager's attention and get the feedback she needed. Do what works best for yourself and those around you to ensure you're on the same page and not spinning on less significant tasks.

Leave your work behind at the end of the work day. Unless you have an on-call job, you don't need to check email constantly; you don't need to respond immediately. I promise all that work will wait for you and be there tomorrow. You will be healthier, refreshed, and more motivated if you take the time for yourself at night.

There will be many times when people push your boundaries. You must learn to say no or communicate what you are willing to tolerate (as well as unwilling to tolerate). If a company or manager does not respect your boundaries, have an open and honest discussion with them to find a solution that meets your needs while still fulfilling your responsibilities. If you are continually pressured to bend your boundaries, it's likely time to start looking for another job with a better culture to support your needs.

When you disregard your boundaries, you set yourself on a path to burnout and future regret about how you've spent your time. Please take this seriously so you don't make the same mistakes I did. At times in my life, it felt easier to turn to work. I was successful at work and knew what I needed to do. That wasn't always the case when dealing with relationships and responsibilities outside of work. For a while, I lost sight of what was most important to me, and my relationships and my health suffered for it. I don't want you to find yourself on that same path.

It's easy to dismiss workplace boundaries on a day-to-day basis, but that day-to-day is your life, and it's imperative to set yourself up for personal and professional success. Say no, put yourself first, and prioritize the things that are most important to you with the time you have in your day and life.

KEY TAKEAWAYS

п Culture can create a supportive work environment that meets your personal and professional goals and values.

п Prioritize work-life balance by aligning your career with your personal values and passions, ensuring that your job supports rather than oversteps your boundaries.

п Implement effective work prioritization methods, like the Eisenhower Method, Rule of Three, or Zero Inbox, to manage tasks efficiently and focus on what's truly important.

п Regularly communicate with your manager to align priorities and adapt to their communication style, if necessary, to maintain focus on significant tasks.

п Set and respect your own boundaries to prevent burnout. Always prioritize personal well-being and relationships over work, and seek a job culture that respects these boundaries.

CHAPTER SIX

DEALING WITH TOXIC CULTURES

Finding oneself in a toxic culture is something I wish no one in corporate ever had to experience. Unfortunately, I've heard countless examples and experienced being caught in a toxic culture or team, recognizing far too late what was happening. Understanding the signs of a toxic culture and its impact on you and those around you while finding a way out are critical skills for anyone in the corporate world. It's also important to be self-aware and ensure you're not contributing to or enabling the toxic environment.

The dynamics of a toxic culture are many, but the end result is anxiety, a loss of productivity, a loss of trust, a loss of confidence, and a loss of direction for those in the environment. Be aware so that you can empower yourself to make the necessary changes to either repair relationships that change the course of the direction of the culture or get yourself out of it.

IDENTIFYING A TOXIC CULTURE

Toxic cultures can exist across entire organizations, within a department, or even within an individual team. While every situation is unique, certain signs can help determine if you are experiencing a toxic workplace. Examples include high turnover rates, a culture of poor communication, a lack of clear career paths or opportunities for promotion, micromanagement, disregard for boundaries, or a generally negative atmosphere that causes a sense of dread about going to work every day.

Many times, people in the midst of a toxic workplace environment have difficulty recognizing it as there is a significant amount of blame on what the problem is, deflection when concerns are raised, or manipulation that, unfortunately, can make us second-guess ourselves.

A manager's micromanagement can cause you to feel like you can never perform or meet expectations. Being constantly critiqued on every move reduces creativity and the ability to take the initiative. A team that doesn't share information transparently can create an environment of mistrust, leading employees to feel in the dark and unsure of the direction or where they can contribute best. An individual constantly asked to disregard their personal commitments in favor of work can quickly become burned out, impacting their overall health.

Like the old example of a frog sitting in a pot, you might notice the water getting warmer but hesitate to jump out. But get out before the water boils over! Reflect on the confidence that you've been working to build and know that there is a better culture that will support your needs elsewhere.

CONVERSATION WITH CARMEN STRATTON, SENIOR MANAGER

Regardless of the scenario, a toxic workplace can negatively affect your career and well-being. It can stifle your professional growth with uncertainty about your next career move. It can impact your confidence and cause you to second-guess what value you can deliver to your team and company. It can also fracture personal relationships when boundaries are crossed and work takes priority. Understanding the signs of a toxic environment is essential to making the most of both your career and the one life that you have. Carmen Stratton, Senior Manager, offers personal insights into identifying and navigating a toxic culture.

What were some red flags when you found yourself in a toxic workplace environment?

Carmen Stratton: I worked for a boss who was prone to yelling whenever he was angry or anxious. He would become extremely upset if anything did not work out as he expected, even if it was beyond our control.

As a salaried employee, I was mandated to get to work at 7:30 a.m. and stay until 4:30 p.m. You couldn't be a minute late; if you were, he would call you out or call you to his office. He controlled the environment, so you could only walk in the front door by his office. With a school-age daughter, 7:30 a.m. was earlier than school drop-off, so I had no option but to hire somebody to take her to school each day.

Since leaving that company, I have much more flexibility and control over my schedule and can better recognize the red flags of a toxic workplace.

Were the yelling and anger directed at you?

Carmen Stratton: Yes, and he would punish me for things beyond my control. For example, our industry was manufacturing, and one of our factories made a mistake and shipped something of poor quality. He was so angry he had me fly to Central America and stay at the factory over the weekend to oversee quality control, which wasn't part of my role. It was common for him to go to these types of extremes when he was upset.

I had a family, including an infant, and he didn't care about taking away from my family time to punish me by requiring unnecessary and unplanned travel. I developed severe anxiety due to long trips away from home. Now that I'm no longer in a toxic environment, work travel is more fun and refreshing.

How did this toxic work environment affect your career progression and overall confidence?

Carmen Stratton: Ironically, I had so much fear that it caused me to work even harder. I felt I needed to be perfect to avoid him yelling at me. So, some parts of me just wanted to show him how talented I was. But I lived in fear and had a ton of anxiety.

Did you get recognition for putting in that extra effort?

Carmen Stratton: No. The only recognition was that I didn't get yelled at. My boss also played favorites and chose someone not to like at random. You just needed to make sure you weren't the one he chose because you would be picked on for six months and be sent overseas all the time. When it was someone else's turn, I was always so relieved it wasn't me that I would keep my head down and work hard.

Did you feel trapped?

Carmen Stratton: I knew I needed to get out. But the mistreatment also made me feel like I wasn't good enough for another job.

What finally made you decide to leave?

Carmen Stratton: I expanded my family and had another child. And the HR department wouldn't let me take the three months off. So when I took some time off to spend with my new baby, I received an email saying, "You need to come back, or you are fired." I came back early, and I just cried. My boss sent me overseas when my baby was only 2.5 months old, which did it for me. That was the catalyst that drove me to leave.

What advice would you offer to someone in a similar situation who is hesitant to leave?

Carmen Stratton: Know your self-worth. Be confident in what you know, and don't believe what others tell you. You have to know deep down inside that you are good enough. You're smart enough. You are qualified, and plenty of great jobs are out there for you.

TAKING RESPONSIBILITY FOR THE TYPE OF WORK ENVIRONMENT YOU ARE CREATING

If you're in a management position, it is crucial to be self-aware and ensure you're not contributing to an unhealthy workplace. Strive to build a culture of transparency and belonging with your team. Share as much information with your team as possible, and give them clear career paths and answers to how they can grow. It is unlikely that your team will be the one to tell you if you aren't living up to their expectations. You'll need others around you to share that feedback, and you must be willing and open to listening and making a change. If you've contributed in any way to building a culture of distrust or hurt among your team, make amends regardless of whether it was unintentional. The perception that you are challenging to work with or creating a difficult environment for your team can impact your working relationship with those around you. And it's up to you to do something about it.

> *"If you want people to believe the system is fair and effective, it's essential to be tough on the most powerful, profitable, and well-known jerks. If you enforce the rule only with the weak performers, people who are easily replaceable, or who deliver bad news and have the gumption to disagree with superiors—and you allow powerful assholes to run roughshod over anyone they please—people will smell your hypocritical bullshit from a mile away."*
> - Robert I. Sutton, *The Asshole Survival Guide: How to Deal with People Who Treat You Like Dirt*

It's also up to you to address people who create a toxic environment within your team. An employee who creates chaos or a poor performer you're not willing to deal with can create a toxic environment just as easily as a bad manager. You are responsible for maintaining a safe environment for all people to work in.

KNOWING WHEN TO LEAVE

> *"In a chronically leaking boat, energy devoted to changing vessels is more productive than energy devoted to patching leaks."*
> -Warren Buffett

Recognize when you're in an unhealthy environment and get out of it to give the right amount of energy to the places in your life that follow your passions and matter the most. The first step is to make a plan. Perhaps the issue is simply the team you're on, and the company culture is otherwise good. If so, you can begin applying and networking for other roles in the company. If your boss won't support the move, HR should help you. But if you aren't getting the help there either, it's time to look outside your current company.

Just as you would with any job search, begin reaching out to your network, updating your resume, and looking for the next suitable position for you. Protect yourself in the interim by practicing self-care and having a solid support system as you continue to look for another job while dealing with a toxic environment. When dealing with a demoralizing work environment, get external perspectives and advice to maintain a clear view of your career goals and your personal worth. If it begins to become too much, remember that you have options such as FMLA or short-term disability to bridge the gap while you make a plan to get out.

You are in charge. Remind yourself of your overall career and life goals. No toxic environment is worth staying in. Take care of yourself and take action to find a new team and workplace that supports your ambitions and well-being. You will never regret making that change.

> *"Sometimes giving up is the strong thing.*
> *Sometimes to run is the brave thing.*
> *Sometimes walking out is the one thing*
> *that will find you the right thing."*
> - Taylor Swift in "It's Time to Go" from Evermore

KEY TAKEAWAYS

஧ Recognize the signs of a toxic culture: high turnover, poor communication, micromanagement, and a negative atmosphere.

஧ Trust your instincts; if you feel uneasy or anxious about your workplace, take action to address the situation.

஧ Don't tolerate mistreatment or disregard for personal boundaries. Prioritize your well-being and seek support if needed.

஧ Self-awareness is key to ensuring you're not contributing to or enabling a toxic environment as a manager or team member.

஧ Know your worth and have the confidence to leave a toxic workplace.

CHAPTER SEVEN
LEADING OTHERS

Leading a team involves growing individuals' careers, building their confidence, recognizing their accomplishments, providing critical feedback, and dealing with the dynamics of interpersonal relationships. Being a leader means handling different personalities, miscommunications, and conflicts, whether between your team members or interactions with other teams. Your feedback and support are key to allowing your team and you to achieve the strongest results and most successful outcomes possible.

You set the stage for how your team, particularly your leadership, behaves within and outside your organization. How you set the stage determines how they will interact with other people, represent you, and approach difficult situations and conversations across the organization. In the following sections, I'll explain how being clear, authentic, and collaborative encourages a team culture that would make any leader proud.

BE AUTHENTIC

One of the keys to being a leader is authenticity. Regardless of the leaders above you or the examples you've seen in your career, becoming a strong leader who people will remember, refer to, and want to work for requires authenticity. There is the potential to get caught up in the ego game of believing that you now know more because you have reached a certain level. But that's not accurate nor a characteristic of a true leader.

There's always room for learning and growth, and the best way for you to grow in your team is to be authentic with them. Engage with them, collaborate with them, encourage dissenting points of view, be curious, and be open to new ideas and continuous learning. Of course, you have much to offer as a leader but also much to learn. Be authentic with your team in the areas you feel confident in and where you want honest feedback and collaboration.

Building connections, being authentic, and being clear will give you a long-lasting reputation as the type of leader people want to work for and work with.

CLEAR IS KIND, UNCLEAR IS UNKIND

"Clear is kind, unclear is unkind." This is one of the best sayings I heard in my career. Articulating what you mean and being precise is much more valuable than being unclear or saying nothing. In reflection, there were a number of times in my career that I was unkind by not saying enough, being unclear, and not giving people the feedback they needed to improve. It is important to understand the value of being clear early, frequently, and authentically when leading a team.

Your people's growth and career opportunities are in your hands as a leader. If you turn that around to yourself, think about how much you would like to know what is holding you back from growing, holding you back from success, or holding you back from being the best that you can be in your career journey. Now consider these from your employees' perspectives. They all want the same feedback.

Remember, don't make assumptions about what they want; your job as a leader is to ensure they can be the best versions of themselves. Your goal is to build them up, recognize their accomplishments, and support them on their career journey. This means giving critical feedback when it's needed. It also means sometimes having awkward, challenging, and uncomfortable conversations to ensure you are clear and providing your employees with the necessary feedback.

Clear is kind. While it may feel uncomfortable in the moment, it allows your employees to improve, grow, and understand how they can do better. Without your feedback, you limit their success and hinder their ability to reach their full potential.

FREQUENT FEEDBACK

You may be thinking, "How do I provide this type of feedback?" I recommend setting aside a quarterly time for this authentic conversation. Remember the "compliment sandwich," where you provide feedback that's needed for areas to improve while also recognizing the employee's accomplishments and how much you appreciate having them on your team. These sessions do not need to be long; I recommend 30 minutes so that you can share their recent accomplishments, critical feedback, and improvements you'd like to see.

Also use this time to understand their concerns, reaffirm your understanding of their career goals, and set any expectations for the next quarter. Then, document these in an email as a follow-up. It's the best way for your employees to understand your expectations. It can also be invaluable if an employee is unwilling to do the work or meet expectations. Underperforming employees are another area where HR can be an incredible source of support.

PARTNERSHIP WITH HR

Every company has different strengths or limitations regarding leaders' partnership with their HR team. In some companies, HR can be a leader's best partner when leading a team. In others, connecting and getting the support you need can be difficult. Regardless of your company, it's important to know which type of HR partner you have so that you can address challenges and obtain support in the best way possible for yourself and your team.

In companies where HR is your partner, it is critical to make the connection and build the relationship. Your HR partner can help you tackle numerous challenges, brainstorm ways to encourage team growth, address criticism, and work through different personality conflicts.

However, when HR is not a strong partner, the onus falls more heavily on you as a leader to find support. Don't go it alone! Look for external resources from HR professionals in your network, your manager, or mentors inside or outside your company. By making these connections, you'll gain access to a network of individuals who can support and brainstorm on the issues a strong HR team would typically handle.

WHEN HR HAS YOUR BACK

When HR is your partner, you have backup in the ring. Someone will help you stand up, dust yourself off, and return to the fight. HR can be one of the most powerful partners for you as a leader. They can help you understand inequality, career growth, and opportunities for those on your team. And they can help you through some of the most complex circumstances for your team members.

These circumstances can be as common as mitigating conflict between team members or other teams to handling complex personal scenarios where you have to determine if or how to support your employees best when they are going through a personal crisis. All of these are challenging, but HR professionals have seen almost everything or at least know how to obtain the information to guide you toward the right solution.

When leading a team, there are many times when you're not dealing with black and white; you're dealing with gray. HR is a fantastic partner to support your team, your team's goals, the company, and most importantly, the individual.

ENCOURAGE COLLABORATION

Always remember that a leader is not synonymous with a dictator. You are there as a leader, and as a leader, that means that you need to lead and respect the team that you have. To truly lead a team, you must encourage collaboration, be curious, ask questions, and build a culture of teamwork and support for one another. Listen to your team, encourage respectful dissent, and always be willing to debate new ideas. The final decision often comes to you, but explain why you've made that decision, respect that others may have different points of view, and acknowledge their contribution.

As mentioned earlier, authenticity is the most important aspect of being a leader; collaboration with your team is a close second. Your openness to collaboration and discussion with your team leads to a stronger team culture and allows your leaders to collaborate more openly. Instead of enabling a toxic team environment where people constantly compete for the best idea or your attention, you value their collaboration for mutual success. This builds a healthy framework for them to collaborate with those outside their team and overcome potential toxic behaviors by supporting one another.

Leaders play a crucial role in guiding their teams towards success. By providing honest feedback, being true to oneself, and encouraging teamwork, leaders can cultivate a positive work environment conducive to growth and achievement. Leadership is not just about making decisions; it's about empowering others and creating a culture of mutual respect.

KEY TAKEAWAYS

ය Authenticity is key to gaining trust and respect as a leader; be genuine in your interactions with your team.

ය Clear communication is crucial; be honest and provide constructive feedback to foster improvement.

ය Establish a strong partnership with HR to navigate challenges and support team growth effectively.

ය Encourage collaboration and value diverse perspectives to build a cohesive and successful team culture.

CHAPTER EIGHT

CREATING A CULTURE OF BELONGING

A leader who can create a culture of belonging will, in turn, create a rewarding workplace where people want to pursue their passions and contribute at high levels to the overall organizational goals. Supporting diversity, equity, and inclusion is not just a platitude or a checkbox; it is making the workplace an environment where everyone feels safe to contribute, engage, and feel a sense of belonging.

The difference between toxic workplaces and workplaces that support a culture of belonging is enormous in terms of employee well-being and company results. Leaders should note what it means to have a well-performing team that feels supported, included, and free to contribute to the incredible results that can be driven within a team and across an organization.

Individuals should look for teams and organizations that curate this type of culture. Through the conversations below, you can get a sense of what it means to create a culture of belonging, the importance of diversity, equity, and inclusion in that culture, and the role that every individual and leader plays in building the type of workplace people want to be a part of.

CONVERSATION WITH CARLIN POWER, GLOBAL SENIOR DIRECTOR, TECHNOLOGY

What does diversity, equity, and inclusion mean to you, and why is it important?

Carlin Power: My approach to DEI is centered on how you show up and what actions you take to make sure everyone you are responsible for, either as a manager or as a partner, has the accessibility and the safety to contribute to your business. If you search the internet, you will get 100 different definitions of what diversity, equity, or inclusion means, but it should be treated like a practice rather than an initiative or a program that you roll out. There are certainly places for employee resource groups from a bottom-up perspective about how they contribute to your company's overall vision. But I teach DEI as a practice. And teach people how people show up.

When people talk generally about diversity, conversations tend to default to race and gender. When I think about diversity, I ask myself a series of questions like, "Have I set up meetings in a way where every person, regardless of who they are and their background and experience, feels like they can contribute based on their strengths, experience, and background?" "Am I attracting the right talent? Is the language I'm using in my job descriptions inclusive?" The answers to these questions force you to look at problems differently. When building diverse teams, I gravitate toward people with the most varied experience so that we can tackle the whole problem. I do not want people to come to the table with the same solutions or fall victim to group-think. We fail ourselves if we do that. And when you have people who have had to navigate things differently because of their circumstances, and you encourage those perspectives in the conversation, you get better results every time.

In terms of equity, I lean heavily into pay equity and accessibility in this space. As a manager, it is my responsibility to make the roles within my team accessible to everyone and to pay people equitably for the work they do. When we are structuring our organizational design, we ask, "Is it transparent and visible on how to move up or through the team?" Is the role we are creating accessible in the organization? Who is excluded as we add qualifications? Are there learning supports in place to close role and qualification gaps?" And if the answer to any of those is no, we know we have to adapt our design strategy.

To close some of those gaps, we've built apprentice programs and partnered with our talent acquisition team to identify missed opportunity markets or places where learning support would close the gap between varied educational backgrounds.

But there is also a dimension of equity in retaining and engaging the people already in your organization. How do you give visible and attainable opportunities to everyone on your team? Examples you can build into your practice are learning academies and stretch assignments, ensuring that everybody has equitable access to stretch assignments to build into their portfolio of projects to prepare themselves for the next level. Also, we assign mentorships as more of a requirement and a standard rather than a privilege.

So why are those practices important? If you are actively involved with career growth and continuously matching people with opportunities, whether it's a lateral move, a change of environment, or getting assigned to a mentor, those intentional redirections turn into predictable retention. Equity is about more than just doing the right thing. It is a business advantage because attrition and disengagement are expensive, and these strategies mitigate that risk and cost.

Pay equity is another issue that comes up a lot. A common dilemma is, "Oh, I'm going to lose this person if I don't give them substantially more base pay." But the truth is, you will lose credibility and trust across the team if you pay people differently for doing the same work. And you absolutely want to retain your highest performers, but that should be covered by discretionary compensation, like bonuses. That should not be built into people's salary and wealth; it should be normal practice.

Inclusion and belonging are harder to measure. And if you're not doing the first two well, true inclusion is largely unattainable. If people don't feel like they can contribute in meetings or feel equitably paid, or if we're not being intentional about their engagement or celebrating their value, they won't feel connected to the organization. Managers can create inclusion through the words they use and actions they role model, which helps, but the hardest thing about inclusion is that everyone has to be bought in.

I recommend doubling down on self-educating and understanding how to include and role model mutual respect for everyone within your organization, actively learning and being transparent and vulnerable about that, and admitting mistakes when they happen. Then everybody else in your sphere of influence develops those same behaviors. And if you celebrate the behaviors that are done well, a project that was delivered inclusively, or a team that came together to solve a problem, it highlights the

SHAWNA MARTIN

behaviors that are important to leadership, which gets repeated. This is how culture is built.

DEI is how you show up and how you practice, whether in your personal life or at work. And it is a journey, not a destination. Your commitment to learning and developing it as a practice, like your functional area of expertise, will make you a much better leader and will help your organization develop a real culture of inclusion.

If you are evaluating a company to work for, how do you determine if it has a culture of inclusion?

Carlin Power: If you are looking for a job and reading a job description, the first thing to look for is if the company uses inclusive language. Did they intentionally go through and reflect their company's values in their job description? Or are they using charged language that may disengage different parts of the population? "Stakeholder" is a word that you might see in a job description that would be disengaging for the Black community. Look for companies that intentionally use inclusive words that reflect the values that resonate with you. That tells me that they've put a lot of thought into the people they want, which will reflect the culture that shows up.

The second thing to consider is the questions asked during the interview process. They should be asking you about inclusive behaviors. For example, "Can you provide an example of a time when you actively sought out diverse opinions or perspectives to drive innovation or solve a complex problem?" "Tell me about a situation where you encountered a cultural or communication barrier in the workplace and how you handled it." Their questions will indicate if collaboration, respect, and inclusion are important to them. You should ask about their DEI practices directly if it doesn't come up during the interview. Whether that management layer feels connected to and can articulate the vision is very telling.

If you are in a current role and want to do more, ask for career plan guidance and tools. A company invested in the progression of all people should be able to give you very clear and transparent plans, programming, and tools to help you get there. When it gets muddy, the path isn't clear, there's little visibility, or it's very vague; this indicates they haven't spent time thinking about retention and accessibility of roles, which is foundational in companies built around inclusion.

I love what you said about DEI being a practice rather than a program. Everyone in the company is responsible for fostering that kind of culture and environment.

Carlin Power: I read a book by Lily Zheng called *DEI Deconstructed* that discusses the different types of roles and responsibilities contributing to a work environment where practicing DEI is normalized. It talks about using your spheres of influence to advocate for people. You need sponsors with formal authority to prioritize DEI, hold others accountable, and evaluate them against it. You need advocates to inspire and energize the centers of gravity of the organization around changing behavior. You need builders who know how to build and operationalize processes that allow inclusion and equitable business practices to run. And each person plays a role. Even if you feel like you don't impact the whole, you *do*, and running DEI as a practice is only possible with every single person having a strength and a role to play. And you need every single one; otherwise, it can't work. So, my advice to anyone reading this is to be really aware of your sphere of influence and use it for good. Your words matter whether you influence one person or thousands of people. Your behaviors matter. You, as an individual, matter.

CONVERSATION WITH NASHUNDA WILLIAMS, GLOBAL HEAD OF DIVERSITY, EQUITY, AND INCLUSION

Why is diversity, equity, and inclusion important? Why should these concepts matter to everyone in the workplace, regardless of their background or role?

Nashunda Williams: Diversity, equity, and inclusion are essential in creating an environment where individuals from all backgrounds and experiences can thrive. Inclusion involves pulling everyone into the conversation of listening, respect, and shared learning – which fosters the most innovative ideas for business success, which should be important to all employees.

The culture of a workplace also matters. It's the result of small, everyday interactions where differences are valued, people feel they belong, and authenticity thrives. If we unlock every employee's potential, any business's future is limitless.

What role do leaders play in fostering a culture of inclusion and belonging for their teams?

Nashunda Williams: Leaders within an organization have an important role in cultivating a culture of inclusion and belonging for their teams. This requires active listening, seeking to understand, and empathy to promote all voices and perspectives.

Leaders who intentionally prioritize inclusion often build high-performing teams. Being humble when needed is an essential part of inclusive leadership. Words like "I didn't know, I am here to learn" or strategically turning an uncomfortable moment into a learning moment – pulling everyone in where someone feels left out is fostering an environment of belonging.

Given your broad, global perspective, are there any best practices, initiatives, or programs that have been effective in your teams or company?

Nashunda Williams: Strategic focus and vision strengthen organizations; best practice is to treat this space like you would any other priority initiative; vision, strategic focus, and objectives are key to successful outcomes. While high-level vision/strategies can be set globally, their execution is diverse, respecting local cultural norms and granting freedom within a framework. In addition, innovation solutions are often found within the employee base; seeking their opinions and perspectives unveils diverse insights necessary for cultivating a world-class culture.

For example, I encountered the challenge of the team functioning individually rather than collectively. As we discussed this topic as a team, it became clear that the team didn't know each other well enough to collaborate closely, especially given their diverse geographic locations. To address this, I asked the team for ideas on fostering connectivity. Out of that discussion came "The Weekly Conversation" – a 30-minute gathering where we discuss non-work topics. We rotate who leads the call, and this small concept has led to great memories for the team and, most importantly, a better sense of connectivity and working relationship, resulting in improved overall performance. Additionally, we now have a template for others to develop their team connectivity across the organization. Discover what works, document, operationalize, and share it openly.

BEING INTENTIONAL IN CREATING A CULTURE OF BELONGING

As we've learned from the conversations with Carlin Power and Nashunda Williams, creating a culture of belonging is not just a program to be rolled out but a continuous practice that demands active participation from everyone within the company. Leaders play a pivotal role in modeling these behaviors, fostering an environment where everyone feels valued, heard, and included. By prioritizing DEI, organizations can unlock the full potential of their teams, driving innovation and achieving superior results. The journey toward a truly inclusive workplace is ongoing, requiring us to contribute, learn, and grow together. By doing so, we create a culture of belonging and pave the way for a more equitable and thriving future for all.

KEY TAKEAWAYS

❧ Diversity, equity, and inclusion (DEI) are not just organizational buzzwords but practices that require active engagement and commitment from every team member, from leadership to individual contributors.

❧ Creating a culture of belonging requires ongoing efforts in equity and inclusion, ensuring everyone has equal access to opportunities and feels valued for their unique contributions.

❧ Leaders have a significant impact on fostering an inclusive environment by modeling respectful behavior, being intentionally inclusive in their actions, and reflecting on their practices to continually improve the culture of belonging within their teams.

❧ Pay equity, mentorship, and accessible career advancement opportunities are essential components of an equitable workplace, directly contributing to higher employee engagement and retention levels.

❧ Inclusion is the culmination of effective diversity and equity practices, where every individual feels respected, valued, and empowered to contribute to the organization's success.

PART THREE

CONNECTION

CHAPTER NINE

THE POWER OF CONNECTION

I always viewed networking as a necessary evil—a checkbox on the career journey. But over time, I've realized that the real magic is in genuine connection. Connection isn't just about swapping business cards or making small talk. It's about getting to know the people around you—your peers, direct reports, and senior managers. It's about being curious about them as individuals beyond just the tasks at hand.

Small talk about the weather or weekend plans can be a good icebreaker, but the deeper your connections, the more meaningful they become. Think about it: in times of need, who would you reach out to for help finding a job—a colleague you've only ever discussed work with or someone you've shared coffee chats and personal stories with? These relationships foster a supportive community where everyone is invested in each other's success.

Building meaningful relationships in the workplace makes every day a little brighter. Your colleagues become your support system, cheerleaders, and sometimes lifelong friends. Whether celebrating wins or weathering challenges, having strong connections in the workplace can make all the difference in your overall happiness and fulfillment.

Connection also helps break down barriers and misunderstandings. When you have strong relationships with your colleagues, addressing conflicts, having difficult conversations, and providing constructive feedback is easier. Instead of making assumptions or jumping to conclusions, you can approach challenges with empathy and a genuine desire to understand the other person's perspective. This open dialogue fosters a culture of honesty and growth within your team and organization.

HOW TO STRENGTHEN CONNECTIONS

The best approach to strengthening connections is to schedule one-on-one meetings with your colleagues—whether in person or virtually. These personal conversations allow for more authentic interactions and deeper connections. If you're a team leader, encourage your employees to set up coffee chats with each other. Similarly, if you are a senior leader, you can set up skip-level meetings with people on the teams beneath your direct leaders. Not only does this give them exposure and an opportunity to meet you as a senior leader, but it also gives you a chance to understand more about what those in your embedded teams do, what their passions are, and how they feel about the company, their manager, and their work.

You might wonder what to discuss in these skip-levels or coffee chats. This is where curiosity wins the game. And I promise it's not that hard, even if it may feel uncomfortable the first few times. Ask questions about how they got into this line of work, what they enjoy about their job, and hobbies. Feel free to ask about family,

SHAWNA MARTIN

and it's okay to ask about vacations if it helps you learn more about them. I recommend staying away from politics, religion, or any other controversial topics.

It's best to avoid focusing the conversation on the status of work projects or venting about what you don't like about the company. The purpose is to get to know the person on the other side of the call to build a relationship. Then, the next goal is to sustain it. That doesn't mean you need to meet every week or month. But check-in; if you're on a group call, ask briefly about a topic you discussed on the coffee chat before the call starts. Send a note in your email for your project status, mentioning that you hope they've had fun doing whatever their favorite hobby is. And still set up follow-up one-on-ones, even if only every six months. It's not about how often but the quality of your connection.

Other ideas for team leaders include virtual or in-person events. Many of us got sick of virtual events during Covid, and rightfully so as they felt forced. However, when events are planned with care and focus on strengthening the connections of a team, they can be incredibly powerful, whether in person or virtually. My favorite virtual events for teams I've led include virtual escape rooms and virtual quiz bowls. Learning how other people work, communicating, and creating friendly competition can help engage the team when they collaborate for work.

When planning in-person events, make sure to have a variety over time so everybody feels comfortable joining. Not everyone is up for a happy hour or parties, so plan lunch or activity-focused events. One of my favorite team events was going to the aquarium in Atlanta during a conference. We had so much fun going through the aquarium, taking silly pictures, hanging out, and laughing; it's a night I'll never forget.

BUILDING CONNECTIONS THROUGH COLLABORATION

Throughout your career, you'll encounter countless opportunities to build connections by collaborating and supporting others' journeys. These opportunities can arise organically: working on projects together, cheering on your team's development, or volunteering to mentor colleagues. These connections not only foster authentic relationships but also empower and elevate the careers of those around you.

Mentorship is a personal favorite for fostering connection, benefiting both the mentor and mentee. If you haven't yet connected with a mentor, tap into your network! Seek someone whose expertise and career path resonate with yours or someone you admire and want guidance from. As you progress in your career, remember to pay it forward by offering mentorship. Consider mentoring someone within your organization or collaborating with HR or external programs to find a mentee match.

Supporting others' careers also involves highlighting their achievements, celebrating their wins, and cultivating a culture of mutual support within your team and organization. This might be as simple as acknowledging a recent accomplishment during a team call, emailing their manager praising their contribution to a project, or submitting a formal recognition through an HR system. Regardless of the method, supporting others' careers strengthens genuine connections that can last throughout your career or even a lifetime.

KEY TAKEAWAYS

ೞ Genuine connection in the workplace transcends mere networking, fostering supportive communities and meaningful relationships.

ೞ Strong connections contribute to career advancement, personal happiness, and overall fulfillment.

ೞ Intimate conversations through coffee chats and skip-level meetings nurture deeper connections and understanding among colleagues.

ೞ Curiosity drives meaningful interactions; ask about interests, passions, and personal stories to build rapport.

ೞ Collaborating and supporting others' careers fosters genuine connections, empowers colleagues, and cultivates a culture of mutual support.

CHAPTER TEN

INFLUENCE WITHOUT AUTHORITY

Many times in your corporate career, you will need to drive an outcome without the appropriate authority to enforce it. This is more common in most corporate life than it is to drive decisions *with* authority. And honestly, who wants to be the dictator who forces everybody to go along with what they want? In comes the ability to influence without authority. Much of this relates to the power of connection that we spoke about earlier, but there are other tips from a coach's perspective that I always offer when people are struggling to get work done across various teams, opinions, personalities, and approaches.

TIPS FOR INFLUENCING

Use the Power of Connection

Make sure that you get to know the team members outside of your direct authority—or even outside your manager's direct authority.

Take time to meet with them one-on-one, have coffee, ask their opinions, and, most importantly, listen.

Find Common Ground with Stakeholders

Find stakeholders who will support ideas you plan to propose in a group setting. It is hard to go into a group when others have different opinions, and it can be overwhelming to present or speak up with your ideas without knowing how people at the table will react. I suggest meeting with one or two people and talking through your idea, gaining their feedback, and determining if they agree with your approaches before presenting at the meeting. Confidants or supporters go a long way when introducing new ideas.

Master the Art of Storytelling

Another approach to influencing without authority is mastering the art of storytelling. Storytelling helps others understand the journey that led to your point of view, presented in the simplest terms possible, and effectively frame your proposal for solutions or next steps.

Here's how it works: Start by focusing on the "why"—the underlying goal or challenge everyone is facing. Then, reframe the problem statement in a clear and concise way. Leverage your strength in connecting with different teams and people. Share various solutions you've gathered through these connections, demonstrating the breadth of your consideration. Finally, use the gathered information, established criteria, and desired outcomes to recommend a specific solution. Briefly explain why this option appears to be the best fit for the situation.

This approach showcases your ability to see the bigger picture and synthesize information from diverse sources. By presenting multiple options before your recommendation, you avoid appearing overly prescriptive and foster a sense of collaboration.

Then, it is equally important to open the discussion to alternative ideas. Sometimes, this can be hard when you have an over-talker at the table who only wants to hear themselves speak. But again, this is where your behind-the-scenes supporter can help stop the conversation and redirect it back on course by soliciting others' opinions in the room.

One of the companies I worked at had a value I appreciated: simplify and edit. The idea was to get across the point with the fewest words possible and the most clarity in those words. Presenting an idea through numerous slides containing excessive details and facts will overwhelm your audience and not effectively express your point. Focus on the storytelling steps above to highlight only the key points of your presentation and share the proposed outcome. When everybody understands the clear "why," problem statement, options, and solution, you can then bring in the appropriate backup details as the group debates solutions. Putting it all on the table up front distracts people from the important discussion and removes the needed conversation that has to occur to build consensus towards the final decision.

Help Drive a Decision Forward

Finally, it is critical to help drive a decision forward. The best way to do this is to go around the room either in the discussion or afterward to get a response from everybody on their opinion of the best path forward. Doing this ensures everyone feels heard and can identify any potential concerns early on. Knowing the ultimate decision maker to whom you're presenting this solution is also essential. It might often be outside of your direct team; however, the final decision maker will look at you and the peers around you to recommend a solution based on all of the different factors and opinions at the table.

Driving a solution forward means that you have clear agreement from those in the room on the best path forward and that you've sought their opinion and feedback before making the recommendation. Remember, the recommendation doesn't always have to be clear-cut, especially when relying on influence rather than direct authority. You can say that the team had two recommendations based on different points of view, lay out the pros and cons, and provide them to the leadership team or whoever is ultimately responsible for making the decision.

By prioritizing connection, finding common ground, and mastering the art of storytelling, you can effectively drive outcomes and foster collaboration across teams. Brevity and clarity are key, and moving decisions forward hinges on collaborative consensus-building. In the influence space, success lies not in having power over others but in fostering relationships and facilitating meaningful dialogue.

KEY TAKEAWAYS

ⓒ Prioritize building connections beyond your immediate sphere of authority, fostering understanding and trust through one-on-one engagement and active listening.

ⓒ Identify stakeholders who align with your proposed ideas beforehand to gain support and confidence in presenting them within group settings.

ⓒ Master the art of storytelling to convey ideas persuasively. Start with the "why," frame the problem, and offer solutions backed by rationale.

ⓒ Embrace brevity and clarity in communication, adhering to the "simplify and edit" principle to ensure the focus remains on productive discussion.

ⓒ Drive decisions through collaborative consensus-building, seeking input from all stakeholders and understanding the decision-making hierarchy.

CHAPTER ELEVEN

NAVIGATING DIFFICULT CONVERSATIONS

No matter how great your job, manager, or workplace environment may be, there will come a time when you face a challenging conversation. Most of us tend to shy away from such situations, hoping to skirt the discomfort they bring. However, as inevitable as they are, these conversations present opportunities for growth and connection within the workplace.

When you embrace the importance of addressing difficult topics head-on, you empower yourself to communicate more effectively, confidently, and authentically with your colleagues. Just as we emphasize the importance of clarity when leading teams, the same principle holds true in handling difficult conversations. Remember: clear communication is an act of kindness, while ambiguity can lead to unnecessary confusion and misunderstandings.

THE COST OF AVOIDANCE

Difficult conversations frequently arise in interactions between peers, managers, employees, and across different organizational teams and levels. These challenges can stem from various sources, including personality conflicts, discrepancies in goal alignment, differences of opinion on problem-solving approaches, or simply miscommunications that have spiraled into larger issues.

Effectively navigating these conversations isn't merely a matter of personal comfort—it's crucial for the health and success of the organization as a whole. When professionals shy away from addressing emotionally charged topics, they can erode trust and hinder organizational outcomes. As Patrick Lencioni states in The Motive: Why So Many Leaders Abdicate Their Most Important Responsibilities, "One of the main responsibilities of a leader is to confront difficult, awkward issues quickly and with clarity, charity, and resolve."

Avoidance only exacerbates the problem, leading to mounting frustration, unclear expectations, and subpar team performance. By sidestepping difficult conversations, individuals not only compromise their relationships with those directly involved but also undermine the trust and cohesion of the broader team. On the other hand, embracing these conversations is an opportunity to strengthen connections and foster a culture of trust and transparency within the organization.

NAVIGATING BIG EMOTIONS

Difficult conversations often trigger a range of emotions, from anxiety and discomfort to fear and apprehension. The mere thought of confronting these discussions can elicit a sense of unease, leading many individuals to shy away from them instinctively. Whether it's the fear of confrontation, the unease of challenging others' viewpoints or authority, or the apprehension of potential repercussions, it's entirely normal to experience a wave of emotions when faced with the prospect of a difficult interaction.

To prepare yourself mentally and emotionally for this type of conversation, it's best to approach it with curiosity and empathy rather than entering the discussion to assign blame or prove yourself right. Focus on understanding the root cause of the communication breakdown. A curious stance creates space for the other party to share their perspective openly, resulting in a more constructive dialogue.

I also encourage you to seek support from a trusted confidant who can provide valuable emotional grounding before diving into the conversation. Whether it's a colleague, mentor, or friend, having a sounding board to clarify your objectives and process your emotions can significantly ease pre-conversation jitters. However, it's essential to approach this support system as a source of constructive reflection and guidance rather than simply venting frustrations.

THE VALUE OF ACTIVE LISTENING AND EMPATHY

In the midst of a difficult conversation, active listening and empathy serve as powerful tools for defusing tension and fostering mutual understanding. As you engage in dialogue, prioritize listening attentively to the other person's words, steering clear of directive language that may inadvertently come across as dismissive or confrontational. Instead, strive to reflect back a summary of their sentiments and inquire whether your understanding aligns with their intentions. This simple act validates their perspective and demonstrates your genuine investment in comprehending their viewpoint.

Nonverbal Cues

Nonverbal cues can speak volumes during a conversation, providing insight into the other person's emotional state and receptivity to dialogue. Pay attention to signs of defensiveness, pausing if necessary to address any underlying concerns. Additionally, ensure that your body language conveys openness and receptivity, maintaining eye contact, adopting an open posture, and speaking in a measured, professional tone.

Balancing Empathy with Assertiveness

Asserting your perspective while demonstrating empathy requires a delicate balance of tact and understanding. Start the conversation by acknowledging the disconnect and expressing a genuine desire to collaborate on finding a solution. Frame your inquiries in a manner that invites dialogue rather than assigning blame, using open-ended questions to encourage the other person's participation and insight. Using "I" statements to convey your thoughts and perceptions can help diffuse tension.

DIFFUSING HOSTILITY WITH GRACE

Even the most prepared individuals can be caught off guard by a difficult conversation. When you suddenly find yourself receiving challenging feedback or unexpected criticism, it's essential to remain composed and employ active listening techniques to navigate the interaction effectively.

If things take a hostile or defensive turn, maintain a calm and empathetic demeanor. Acknowledge the emotional intensity of the situation and reiterate your commitment to working together toward a mutually beneficial outcome. Express your appreciation for the person's willingness to engage with you while emphasizing the importance of maintaining a respectful and supportive tone.

In cases where the conversation becomes too overwhelming to navigate independently, I recommend seeking support from a senior leader or HR professional. Bringing in a neutral third party can facilitate a more constructive dialogue and ensure both parties feel heard and respected.

Whether you're a seasoned leader, a dedicated employee, or a supportive peer, confronting complex scenarios is an inevitable part of maintaining productive relationships and driving meaningful outcomes. Remember the guiding principle: Clear is kind, and unclear is unkind. The next time you find yourself facing a daunting conversation, take a moment to center yourself, formulate a plan, and lean into the discomfort. Growth often emerges from adversity, and each challenging conversation is a stepping stone on your journey toward greater resilience, empathy, and connection in the workplace—and beyond.

KEY TAKEAWAYS

ༀ Embrace difficult conversations as opportunities for personal and organizational growth, using clarity in communication to avoid misunderstandings and build trust.

ༀ Prepare for emotionally charged discussions with a mindset of curiosity and empathy, focusing on understanding rather than blaming. Seek support from trusted confidants to process emotions and clarify objectives.

ༀ Employ active listening and empathy during conversations to defuse tension and foster mutual understanding. Reflect on the other person's words and confirm your comprehension of their sentiments.

ༀ Manage nonverbal cues to enhance receptivity and openness, and balance empathy with assertiveness to communicate your perspective.

ༀ When conversations become overly challenging or hostile, maintain composure, use active listening, and consider involving a neutral third party to ensure constructive dialogue and desired outcomes.

CHAPTER TWELVE

GAINING RECOGNITION

Recognition isn't merely about seeking promotions or higher compensation; it's about cultivating appreciation for your contributions within your team and organization. Recognition boosts your emotional well-being and self-esteem and plays a pivotal role in securing your financial stability and paving the path for career advancement. It validates your skills and expertise, instilling a sense of pride in your work and bolstering your enthusiasm to tackle new challenges.

Recognition often translates into tangible rewards such as higher bonuses and salary increases, ensuring that your hard work is fairly compensated. At the same time, it serves as a catalyst for career growth and success by improving confidence and increasing awareness of your skills and expertise within your professional network. Receiving acknowledgment for your contributions, whether on a successful project or through your expertise, solidifies your reputation as a valuable asset. Peers turn to you for advice and support, while leaders entrust you with crucial responsibilities, paving the way for further advancement and promotion.

This enhances your negotiating power for compensation, bonuses, and opportunities.

Effectively communicating your unique strengths is essential for standing out among your peers and gaining the recognition you deserve. While you might hope that recognition naturally follows successful projects, it often requires proactive efforts on your part to highlight your accomplishments and expertise. In a workplace where recognition may be lacking, strive to advocate for yourself by showcasing your achievements, skills, and contributions. You might wonder how to do this without projecting arrogance or self-centeredness. Here are some techniques to bring attention to your accomplishments gracefully:

1. **Create a Brag Box:** Establish a "brag box" to compile instances of recognition, appreciation notes, and successes you've received throughout the year. This can be a folder in your email inbox where you store emails of gratitude or praise from colleagues, clients, or supervisors. Save these acknowledgments and use them as evidence of your contributions during performance reviews or meetings with your manager.

2. **Offer Recognition to Others:** Lead by example by recognizing and celebrating your peers and team members. Highlighting their successes fosters a culture of appreciation within your workplace and subtly draws attention to your involvement in their accomplishments. Whether through email commendations, public acknowledgments during team meetings, or submitting recognition awards through HR channels, showing support for others can enhance your visibility and reputation.

SHAWNA MARTIN

3. **Utilize Presentation Opportunities:** Take advantage of presentations or meetings to subtly showcase your achievements and contributions. When presenting project summaries or updates, outline the goals and accomplishments achieved thus far before diving into the core content. This approach is a gentle reminder of your contributions without overtly boasting, effectively reinforcing your value to the team or organization.

4. **Foster a Culture of Recognition:** If you're in a leadership position, create opportunities to celebrate individual and collective successes, such as annual recognition presentations or regular updates highlighting team successes. By openly acknowledging and celebrating team members' accomplishments, you boost morale and showcase your leadership skills in nurturing talent.

EXTENDING YOUR REACH

Gaining recognition within your organization is crucial, but extending your reach through professional platforms like LinkedIn is equally important. Keep your LinkedIn profile updated with current information about your career achievements and aspirations. Craft a compelling "About Me" section highlighting your strengths and goals and detailing your most recent role, emphasizing key responsibilities and accomplishments. You can use LinkedIn to share certifications and career milestones. You can also give updates about significant wins, provided they can be shared publicly and aligned with professional norms.

Feel free to request recommendations from colleagues and

clients who can vouch for your skills. Timing is key; ask for recommendations promptly after completing successful projects or transitioning to new roles to capture fresh insights and feedback. Authentic testimonials from trusted connections can enhance your professional reputation.

Additionally, congratulate and promote your connections' successes to support an environment of mutual recognition. Stay engaged with these connections by interacting with posts, joining professional groups, and attending networking events. Cultivate meaningful connections and participate in industry discussions to expand your reach and visibility.

Actively maintaining your presence on professional platforms positions you for future opportunities and networking prospects. Building a solid online presence lets you stay connected with colleagues, mentors, and potential employers, demonstrating your proactive approach to professional growth and recognition. Incorporate these strategies into your routine to maximize your impact and recognition within and beyond your organization.

THE PURSUIT OF RECOGNITION AND PASSION

Pursuing recognition plays a vital role in amplifying the rewards of your efforts. When you align your career path with your passions, being acknowledged for your contributions becomes gratifying and a testament to your dedication and expertise.

Remember that achieving recognition often requires stepping out of your comfort zone and advocating for yourself. It involves confidently highlighting your successes and articulating why you deserve advancement. One of my clients exemplified this by advocating for herself as an individual contributor, showcasing her

SHAWNA MARTIN

accomplishments, skills, and aspirations for a leadership role. Through her proactive approach, she secured a promotion to a leadership position within just one year, presenting her with exciting opportunities to collaborate with senior executives on high-profile projects in the FinTech industry.

By embracing uncomfortable conversations, cultivating opportunities for advancement, and expecting fair compensation, you elevate your professional standing and pave the way for continued growth and success. Recognition validates your dedication and expertise and fuels your motivation to pursue your passions and achieve your career aspirations.

I encourage you to know your self-worth and the value of your contributions. Consider the broader impact of recognition on your work environment. Your actions can shape the culture of your workplace, influencing its dynamics and creating a space where recognition, appreciation, and acknowledgment thrive.

In your quest for this recognition, remember the power of reciprocity. As you seek acknowledgment for your successes, extend the same courtesy to your peers and colleagues. Celebrating their wins strengthens your bonds and contributes to a culture of mutual support and appreciation. Ultimately, recognition is a reflection of collective achievement. Embrace the opportunities to showcase your talents, advocate for your worth, and uplift those around you. Keep striving, growing, and letting recognition fuel your ascent to greater heights in your professional endeavors.

KEY TAKEAWAYS

ↂ Recognition isn't just about promotions or higher pay; it fosters appreciation within teams and organizations, boosting emotional well-being and paving the path for career advancement.

ↂ Tangible rewards like bonuses and salary increases often accompany recognition, solidifying your reputation as a valuable asset and enhancing your negotiating power.

ↂ Effective communication of your value proposition is crucial for gaining recognition; techniques like maintaining a "brag box" and offering recognition to others can help showcase your achievements gracefully.

ↂ Extend your reach beyond the workplace through platforms like LinkedIn, sharing achievements, requesting recommendations, and engaging with professional connections to increase visibility and networking opportunities.

ↂ Aligning your career with your passions and advocating for yourself is vital in achieving recognition and excellence while contributing to a culture of mutual support and appreciation.

SHAWNA MARTIN

EPILOGUE

"In the journey of your career, be the author of your story. Write it with purpose, edit it with resilience, and let success be the final chapter."
~ **Shawna Martin**

Congratulations on reaching the end of this book! By reading these chapters, you've prioritized your personal and professional growth, stepping boldly into your career journey. You've equipped yourself with the knowledge to enhance your confidence in navigating the corporate world, select the right cultural environment, and develop meaningful connections that truly matter.

You now possess the power to recognize your passions and align your career goals accordingly. You've learned to advocate for yourself, fight for fair recognition and compensation, and navigate toxic environments and challenging conversations. This empowerment sets a new trajectory for your career and life.

However, the true value of this knowledge depends on its application. I urge you to use what you've learned to forge the career path you desire, one that fulfills your passions and meets your life's goals. Remember, your career will occupy a substantial part of your life; make it reflect your highest aspirations. Build that confidence, secure your deserved recognition, and remember, you are not alone in this journey.

While this book serves as a mentor in your back pocket, helping you navigate the complexities of a corporate career, it doesn't replace the guidance of a live mentor, advocate, or coach. I encourage you to seek someone to support you throughout your career. If you are looking for more direct support, I am here to help. Consider booking a complimentary Seedling Coach Discovery Session with me to explore how I can assist in your career growth.

As you move forward, keep these key points in mind:

- **Recognition and Compensation:** You deserve recognition and fair compensation for your contributions. Be confident in your abilities as you pursue your passions and career aspirations.
- **Culture and Growth:** Actively seek out or create a workplace culture that nurtures your growth and well-being. If you find yourself in a less supportive environment, have the courage to make a change.
- **Connections and Joy:** The relationships you build are the foundation of your career. Invest in nurturing these connections, as they will bring joy and fulfillment throughout your professional life.

I hope you continue cultivating the confidence, connections, and culture that resonate with you. Be patient with yourself, understanding that while there may be missteps, each step is part of a larger career journey, not a final destination. Surround yourself with the right support, and remember: You've got this!

Ready to cultivate your career? Book a complimentary Seedling Coach Discovery Session and start growing towards your professional goals today.

www.seedlingcoach.com/discovery

SHAWNA MARTIN

ABOUT SHAWNA MARTIN

FOUNDER
SEEDLING COACH

From building career confidence to finding your own way in the corporate world, Shawna Martin is the expert with empathy who can guide you on your way to becoming recognized and rewarded at work. She's led global leadership teams, guided executives on transformative career journeys, and even mentored young adults looking to start on a solid financial footing.

Shawna kicked off her career in technology over two decades ago. Her journey included managing global teams of more than 200 people and budgets exceeding $200 million. Her knack for nurturing talent—and fiercely fostering innovation—naturally evolved into the private coaching practice she is so passionate about today.

As the founder of Seedling Coach, she offers a unique blend of corporate wisdom and compassionate coaching that helps her clients navigate the complexities of the modern workplace to achieve and sustain their professional goals. Her holistic approach is rooted in authenticity and emotional intelligence, creating a safe space for her clients to explore new ideas of what's possible in their work and life.

WHAT SHAWNA'S CLIENTS ARE SAYING...

"Before working with Shawna, my biggest challenge was navigating through a larger organization. I needed to simplify my career goals to make them achievable. This challenge made me feel a little lost and overwhelmed. However, after starting to work with Shawna, everything changed for the better. Shawna, having been in the industry for many years with a large corporation, allowed me to pick her brain and take advice on how to navigate through certain situations with my immediate team and align myself with the broader organizational goals. This collaboration helped me gain success and satisfaction in my role.

I found my grounding in my team and the company, developing the confidence to express my opinions and thoughts. Shawna is a great mentor who can understand your career goals in line with your personal background. Simplifying your thoughts into actionable items will let you achieve your goals. You will always have something to learn from Shawna's experience and ability to understand!"

- Mahitha Voola, Data Scientist, Milwaukee, WI

∼

"Prior to working with Shawna, my absolute biggest challenge was getting the opportunity to move from an individual contributor to a manager role. This left me feeling frustrated because I was acting in a managerial capacity in many ways—taking on responsibility, risk, expectations, and cross-functional projects—without the title and pay.

Working with Shawna brought significant changes. I started feeling more confident in myself, my ability to make decisions, and my ability to lead. It felt like I was finally working in the space I was meant to be in and receiving the respect I had wanted for years. Specific results from our collaboration include moving into a manager role six months after we started working together consistently, a salary increase by 28% within the first year, passing an advanced financial license exam and completing a six-month compliance certification within the first year, and succeeding in 100% of the 20 large goals I set in the last two years. I attribute this significant success to the guidance, requests for updates, and encouragement Shawna gave me during that time.

If you want someone who will hold you accountable, encourage you to push yourself, and plan to achieve goals that seem out of reach today, book a session ASAP. You will be so much farther a year from now by working with Shawna. Shawna, you are amazing, and I love working with you!"

- Alyssa Junk, Manager of Brokerage Testing and
  Monitoring, Denver, CO

~

"Before working with Shawna, I didn't know what I wanted for the next step in my career. I was confused and unsure of my options. However, after working with Shawna, I realized I have options and that it's not about if I *can* take the next step but if I'm *willing* to take the leap. Now, I have more clarity on what I want my career and life balance to be.

Shawna asked all the right questions, which helped me organize my thoughts, and provided links to great resources after every session. I highly recommend Shawna for her ability to clarify and guide."

- Courtney Lehmann, Finance Manager, Global Medical Device Company, Naples, FL

~

"Prior to working with Shawna, I struggled with time management and maintaining a strategic focus. Despite being seasoned in my career, I found it difficult to adjust to change and needed time to recenter myself and my priorities. Working with Shawna introduced me to tools that have significantly helped me recenter and feel more confident in my strategic planning. Regarding time management, completing my Power List at the end of each day, which includes the top 3-5 priorities for the following day, has helped me focus on important work rather than busy work like emails. For strategic focus, Shawna assisted me in developing a mindset based on operational performance goals.

As they say about parenting, it takes a village. Working with a coach like Shawna is one person you will not regret adding to your village."

- Kristina Bernatis, Asset Manager, Real Estate, Plano, Texas